LINEAR TIME MANAGEMENT

The Key to High Personal Achievement!

By

David C Clark

British Library Cataloguing In Publication Data
A Record of this Publication is available from the British Library

ISBN 978-1-84685-809-3

First Published 2007 by
Exposure Publishing,
an imprint of
Diggory Press Ltd
Three Rivers, Minions, Liskeard, Cornwall,
PL14 5LE, UK
and of Diggory Press, Inc.,
Goodyear, Arizona, 85338, USA
WWW.DIGGORYPRESS.COM

This book is dedicated to my wife, Angela,
for all her help, support and advice

and

All those who are struggling to manage their
time, believing that they do not have enough
of it to get everything done

About the Author

David Clark has been developing leaders, teams and individuals since the mid 1980's and has been running his own consultancy since 1991.

He is originally from Zimbabwe, where he was born and educated, and has lived in the UK since 1973.

He is particularly interested in motivation and its use in achieving high performance.

David has been involved with goal setting since he was a teenager, and has used the content of his book to great personal effect.

He is a business coach, life coach and rugby coach. He lives in Cornwall with his wife Angela and three of his five children.

How to use this book.

This book is intended to be used as a workbook, not something to be left on the shelf.

As you read it use highlighters and coloured pens to identify things that are new to you, you consider important, or wish to apply.

The contents and subject matter of the book have all been tried and tested by the author over many years, and they work.

All you have to do is apply them and you too can create the life of your dreams. You are already doing that – the book will help you to get it right in future!

Chapters

Page No.

Preface

1 - In the beginning…   8

2 - What do you really want…   17

3 - Motivation...   37

4 - The Power of the Brain…   52

5 - Linear Time Management …   78

6 - In Conclusion…   100

Whether you think you
can, or whether you think
you can't, you are probably
right!

Henry Ford

Preface

Time, that most valuable of all our resources, yet the one of which we are least aware. With it we can do so much, yet without it we are nothing.

So why do we treat it the way we do?

Why do we let other things take up so much of what we have so little of?

Why do we squander it so fruitlessly yet place such a high value on other less important things?

What we do with our time is our choice.

If you are not making the most of your time and your life, you are missing out. This book is for you. Follow the guidelines and remember that there is only one true success in life, which is to lead your life in your own way.

It's your choice. Just as it always is with everything you do. Choose wisely. Choose well. Choose linear time management as the way forward.

Chapter 1 - In the beginning…..

Have you ever wondered why it is that some people seem to achieve so much more then others? Or why some seem to attract so much more luck than others do?

I know I have wondered both. Luckily for me, in my role as a people developer and personal coach I have been fortunate enough to be able to work with some of these individuals and discover exactly what it is that makes them so different from everyone else.

Now I can share these findings with you.

What is really interesting is that the difference between the two groups has nothing at all to do with:

- Age
- Education
- Intellect
- Social background
- Gender

or any other physical or social
characteristic that differentiates
people.

Ultimately it all comes down to how
effective these individuals are at managing
their time. The way they do this means that
they both enable and empower themselves,
and the result is that they are able to
maximise their personal effectiveness.

The good news is that you too can learn to do
this - if you want to!

So what exactly is "effective" time
management? Unfortunately it is not as
simple as it is portrayed to be in books and
on training courses. It is not simply making
lists of things that need to be done, and
having a go at prioritising them. It is much
more than that, and has a far wider reach than
it might first seem.

Effective time management is a composite
activity, consisting of several parts. Each and
every one of these component parts is
important, and ignoring just one of them will

Like anything else, success has a price. To be successful you have to be prepared to pay the price.

Walter Greenberg

lead to you sabotaging your attempts to succeed.

To begin with, it is important that you know what it is that you want to achieve. Without having a clear idea of that, a lot of your time will be wasted and lost forever.

Once you have a clear idea of what you want, you will find that you are able to benefit from the release of the right type of motivation. There are only two types of motivation, and one of them will bring significant benefits whilst the other will severely hamper you and restrict your performance.

Next you will discover that because you know what you want and are motivated in the right way, you are able to access very powerful areas within your brain that lie dormant until awakened.

The final piece of the jigsaw is the way in which you approach your personal organisation.

Most people see time as one dimensional, which I refer to as "vertical time", and try to run their lives only in this dimension. However there is another dimension, which is that of "linear time".

Those who experience success at the highest levels do so in part because whilst the majority of individuals attempt to manage their time in the vertical dimension only, they in fact are managing linear time, which gives them the edge.

I have named this composite approach "Linear Time Management," and it is the pathway to high levels of personal success.

Success in life however is as much to do with attitude of mind as anything else. That attitude is brought about through personal determination, resilience, integrity and self belief.

We lead our lives as we
imagine them in our minds

Henry David Thoreau

Successful people actually know what they want and go out to achieve it – it is what drives them.

However they are in the minority.

The majority of people are different. They either don't know what they want, or, as can frequently happen, do not believe they are entitled to, or worthy of, high levels of success.

However, unclear as they are about what they do want, these very same people tend to be very good at knowing what they don't want, but only after they have got it!

NOTES: Take a few moments here to gather your thoughts about what you really want out of life. Use the space below to make your notes.

Chapter 2 – What do you really want...

Do you know what it is that you actually want to achieve?

Have you got a clear mental picture of where you would like to be in 5 or 10 years time?

Some years ago, Harvard, one of the top American universities, carried out a survey on the graduating class of a particular year. Amongst all the questions asked of them, one in particular referred to goals.

The graduating students were all asked whether or not hey had any personal life goals and if so how they were recorded and monitored, if at all.

87% of the students in the year confessed to not having any goals, believing that life was a journey with events along the way and that life had to follow its course. What would be would be!

10% of students however admitted to having goals, which they claimed they kept in their heads, and they declared that they fully hoped to achieve them.

The final 3% said that they had very clearly specified goals, which were written down and reviewed on a regular basis.

Some 20 years later, Harvard got in touch with the same people and re-surveyed them, to find out what had happened during the intervening period.

There had been little if any contact during the intervening years, and therefore no preconceived ideas about what to expect.

One of the most interesting things to emerge from the re-survey was that the original 3% who had the written goals and who reviewed them regularly had all done much better in life than the others.

In fact between them they had amassed more earned wealth than the other 97% of students added together.

When things are easy
everyone wants to be
involved. As things get
tougher however, people
start to drop out until only
those with the resolve and
determination to succeed are
left. Only they give
themselves the chance to
succeed.

Reuben Bernstein

The findings of this piece of research are very interesting. They confirm what others have discovered for themselves, and give a valuable insight into approaches to, and the benefits to be gained from, goalsetting.

Of course, it is perfectly OK to "go with the flow" if that is what you choose to do. However, all the evidence shows that in the majority of cases success very rarely comes about by accident. Invariably success comes by design, and the start of that design process is goalsetting.

My involvement in people development over the past 25 years has shown me that very, very few individuals have set themselves challenging life goals in any sort of structured way. I believe that there are two main reasons for this.

The first of these is that they do not understand how important and powerful goalsetting can be, whilst the second is they do not know how to set challenging goals for themselves in a way that can virtually guarantee success.

Probably the hardest part about goalsetting is deciding what it is you actually want to achieve. Once you know what that is however you can then apply a goalsetting "formula" or process to give yourself the best possible chance of achieving it.

That process can be described through the following five steps:

- See It!
- Say It!
- Write It!
- Read It!
- Do It!

If you do each of these five things in the right order, you will find that you can achieve virtually any challenging goal you set yourself. All you have to do is ensure that you do each of them properly.

There is a very thin line
between success and failure.
The energy required to cross
the gap is minimal compared
to the energy required to get
there.

David Clark

See It!

The first step in the goal setting process is to decide what it is you actually want to achieve. It is important to understand that goalsetting only works on what you want, not what you don't want, so you need to be able to define and describe what it is you want.

This involves using your imagination, as you need to be able to imagine the goal in 2 ways. The first of these is to be able to see what it is that you want to achieve. Unless you can see that, you are not going to get very far.

The second thing is that you need to be able to imagine yourself as having already achieved the goal.

The brain can do both of these incredibly well, if you will let it.

In fact, the word "imagine" actually means to "image-in" and it refers to the brains ability to create images of whatever we want it to.

When you use your imagination in the context of goal setting, all that you are doing is bringing into your consciousness an image of your goal in a very specific way, already having been achieved.

We all know that we can replay an experience we have had, reliving it in our minds. We can also "pre-play" an experience or event, in the same way, like a form of mental rehearsal.

In terms of goal setting we need to be able to do this at the outset. We begin by using our imagination to create our goal, in all its glory!

Some of us are visually oriented – that means we see pictures in our imagination. Some however are verbally oriented, which means we describe our goal in words rather than see pictures.

It does not actually matter which your preference is, as long as you do it.

It is really important that you are able to mentally experience your goal as having already been accomplished. For example, if your goal is to own a new coat, then use your imagination to "see" yourself wearing the new coat, and looking good in your new coat. Say you want to buy a new house, don't just see the house – see yourself living in the house, sitting in your new lounge or eating at your table in your new farmhouse kitchen, if that is what you want.

Whatever it is that you want to achieve, you need to be able to see yourself having achieved it to have any chance of success.

This is what we call the power of positive thinking. In simple terms, if you can see it you can have it or be it, but if in your mind you cannot see yourself having achieved it, you are very, very unlikely to do so.

The great thing in this world
is not so much where we
stand but in what direction
we are moving. We must sail
sometimes with the wind,
and sometimes against it,
but we must sail, not drift
nor lie at anchor.

Lord Nelson

Say It!

Once you have completed the first stage, and visualised or verbalised your goal, the next stage is to test your belief in yourself. The reason for this is very simple. If you do not believe that you are capable of achieving your goal, your brain will not be able to help you to achieve it. In fact, your brain will prevent you from achieving it.

We will look at how this works in more detail later in the book. However, the important thing for you to know is that if you cannot convince yourself of your ability to achieve your goal, you will not achieve it.

Interestingly, this is the point at which the majority of individuals fail. They are able to create the mental image of the goal, and then hit the "I can't actually see myself doing that" wall!
At that point all is lost. Our brains only act on what we believe to be true. Therefore, if we do not believe in our ability to achieve our goal, we will not do it!

Write It!

Once the goal is set and we are committed to it, the next stage involves writing it out in all its detail.

It is important that the written goal contains all the detail required to define it clearly and specifically. For example, "to earn more money" is not the same as either "to earn an income of £30,000.00 a year," or "to earn £5,000.00 a year more than I currently earn." Of these last two, however, the first is the more appropriate, as it is a very specific amount.

The other thing that is very important to include in the written goal is a date by which the goal is to be achieved. An open ended goal is not much use at all – there has to be a very specific date for completion.

Goals tend to fall into one of three categories, defined by timescales, and these are defined as short term, medium term and long term.

Men go abroad to wonder at
the height of mountains, at
the vast compass of the sea,
at the Great Plains and
forests, and they pass by
themselves without
wondering at all.

Aristotle

Exactly how these categories are defined is for us as individuals to decide.

Typically however, short term goals would possibly be those we can achieve over the next three to six months. Medium term goals would fit into a period extending from 6 months up to 5 years. Long term goals would be goals that would be achieved from five years onwards.

In fact, many individuals set themselves life-goals, and you may find a visit to the website of an explorer called John Goddard worthwhile, as the story of his life is extremely interesting. You will find it at www.johngoddard.info.

When you sit down to think about your goals think about the different time spans and decide what you want to achieve in all of them. Obviously the bigger more complex goals take more time. Not just that, but these larger goals can be broken down into sub-goals which can be completed along the way over shorter timescales, so remember to do just that and you will be amazed at just what you can achieve.

Read It.

Having set the goal and committed it to paper, the next stage is the review process.

It is important to review it regularly in order to keep yourself on track. It is very easy to put goals to one side in favour of something more pressing, and gradually they fall by the wayside.

To prevent this it is essential to review goals at least once a week, but preferably daily.

There are three main reasons for this.

Firstly, a regular review will act as a refresher or reminder to you. Because of the timescales associated with goals, it is easy for things with a greater sense of immediacy or urgency attached to them to push the goals out of the way, even when the goals are much more important.

The saying "out of sight is out of mind" comes into play here, and regular reviews keep our goals at the forefront of our mind, in our conscious awareness where we can deal with them.

Secondly, we can monitor our progress regularly and take appropriate action to keep us on track. The pursuit of a goal rarely goes smoothly, because there are all sorts of additional internal and external forces and pressures acting on us which can cause us to deviate from our path.

When this happens we need to know, so that we can take remedial action to get back on the track we want to be on.

Finally we are able to monitor the currency and validity of our goals to ensure they are still worthwhile to us.

Destiny is not a matter of chance – it is a matter of choice. It is not a thing to be waited for – it is a thing to be pursued.

Manfred Roxtead

Things change - we change - and there is no point in keeping goals that have lost their importance because of changes that have happened. We can replace them with more meaningful goals.

We also know the brain, particularly the memory, responds well to repetition, and regular reviews can and do have a very powerful effect on our subconscious mind.

Do It!

It does not matter how well you define and record your goals, if you do not take action. Goals do not get achieved by chance – they get achieved because people take action.

There is an allegedly old Chinese proverb that states: "Man stand long time on side of hill with mouth open before portion of crispy fried duck flies in". O.K. so it is someone's idea of humour, but it does make the point rather well.

The secret is to identify what you can do to move you towards the achievement of your goal.

In my personal experience it is often the simplest smallest actions that can have the greatest impact, so look for the things you can do, and don't worry about the things you can't. There is a way and you will find it.

What has been outlined above is the process that those successful Harvard students, and many more like them, used to set and achieve their goals. It worked for them, and it will work for you. All you have to do is use it!

Effective goalsetting is a very powerful tool that can and will bring about powerful results. We are constantly being told that we do not fully understand the brain or that we only use a tiny fraction of its ability.

Goalsetting, done properly, enables us all to harness some of that latent power and use it to create what we want, as we have imagined it in our minds!

Good timber does not grow
with ease

The stronger the wind, the
stronger the trees.

Elsa Cypriani

Chapter 3 – Motivation

Everything that we do in life we do because we are motivated to do it, for one reason or another. Whether we sit still or whether we do a five mile run, it is because that is what we are motivated to do.

Motivation works at several levels. The first of these is what we call needs driven motivation. Needs driven motivation is all about sustaining life. If we are thirsty we are motivated to drink until we no longer feel thirsty. If we are hungry then we are motivated to eat. The same thing applies to sleep and warmth, amongst others.

These sorts of needs are biologically based and the motivation to satisfy them is triggered automatically. There are also psychological needs, like the need to be accepted by others, or the need to be recognised as an individual in our own rights. Whilst the biological needs can be described as fairly simple, the psychological needs are more complex.

When it comes to the psychological needs, many individual factors come into play, such as the level of ambition one individual has compared with another or the differences in the way people value things.

These sorts of issues are to be found reflected in the goals that each individual sets for themself, or even in whether they set goals or not. However there is another perhaps more important aspect to motivation that needs to be addressed and that concerns the type of motivation that an individual experiences.

Essentially there are two different types of motivation.

The first is achievement motivation. Achievement motivation is the physical and psychological energy that is released in order to help us achieve something that we value and desire.

The second type is avoidance motivation, and that is the energy required to avoid danger or potential danger. It is part of our natural survival system, often called our stress mechanism, and provides our flight or fight capability.

Both these types of motivation are associated with our self image, the mental picture of ourself that we carry about in our mind.

The self image really consists of three separate parts. The first of these is the one we call the "actual" self image, a mental image of who we are. The actual self image is what is responsible for our day to day behaviour and performance.

This section of the self image is built up over time and is normally structured around past experiences that we have successfully dealt with.

As such it creates a "comfort" or "safe" zone, which is a psychologically safe and comfortable place to be.

Whenever we face up to a new situation we analyse it very quickly in our mind, and

A dream is just a dream. A goal is a dream with a plan and a deadline.

Harvey MacKay

make a decision as to whether it represents a threat, an opportunity or neither.

If we consider the new situation to be a threat, which will in some way diminish or disadvantage us, we create another version of our self image, called the damaged, or corrupted self image. This is a mental picture of how we will be if we are disadvantaged.

Once we see this, we generate what is known as avoidance motivation, designed to help us deal with the perceived threat, and intended to prevent our self esteem being damaged. Avoidance motivation is about preservation and maintaining what is already in existence. In fulfilling its purpose it has an adverse effect on performance because it can and does:

- Cause convergent thinking, closing down our creativity and thinking ability
- Make us feel victims to circumstances
- Create a negative mindset
- Shake our confidence and disable our abilities

- Diminish us
- Make us reactive to events
- Increases worry and fear

Avoidance motivation has a very important part to play as part of our survival mechanism, specifically in relation to dealing with what we perceive as a threat.

However it is at its best when used in the short term, as prolonged use of avoidance motivation can cause physical and psychological exhaustion, leading to a type of impairment known as stress.

Opportunity on the other hand releases achievement motivation, which works in a different way altogether.

When we are presented with an opportunity, one of the by-products is personal growth or gain, which in turn will enhance the self image and self esteem.

This releases the achievement motivation designed to help us to succeed.

Achievement motivation can enhance performance because it can and does:

- Facilitates personal growth

- Cause divergent thinking which expands the mind and opens up opportunities

- Makes us appear luckier as more existing opportunities are identified

- Creates a "positive mental attitude" via positive expectancy

- Enables us and develops a "can-do" attitude

- Empowers us and increases the confidence we have in ourselves

- Encourages us to be more pro-active wherever we can

Whatever you can do, or
dream you can do, begin it.
Boldness has genius, power
and magic in it.

Goethe

How we identify "opportunities" depends upon the third part of our self image, known as the "ideal" self image. This is a mental picture we have of ourself as we would like to be.

This image is a composite, made up of many parts, and opportunities are defined as events or circumstances that will enable us to move closer to our ideal self.

Unless what is occurring has that capability it is not an opportunity, just a situation.

This ideal self image can be built around tangible and intangible aspects, such as personal development and growth, club membership, cars, income or home ownership.

When we set goals, what we are doing is creating a new self image, to incorporate the completed goal, hence why in the earlier chapter you were encouraged to see yourself as having achieved your goal.

This creates a gap between where we are (actual self image) and where we want to get to (ideal self image).

The purpose of achievement motivation is to provide us with the wherewithal, in the form of physical and mental energy, to close that gap.

As long as the gap exists, and we are determined enough to want to achieve the goal, we will benefit from achievement motivation.

Perhaps a good way to explain how these motivations work is to use the example of change in the workplace.

The modern world is continuously changing, especially in the workplace. Imagine then the situation that arises when an individual is both competent and comfortable in their role, possibly as a result of the many years of

If you have built castles in
the air, your work need not
be lost - that is where they
should be. Now put
foundations under them.

Henry David Thoreau

experience in the job, and is suddenly faced with change.

The change may represent a threat to the nice comfy life they are leading, which does not require any real effort on their part. If this is the case, then it may trigger avoidance motivation, interpreted as resistance to change, designed to preserve and maintain what they already have.

Now let's look at another individual in the same organisation, someone who is ambitious and keen to get on. For this individual change represents an opportunity, a chance for them to move towards their ideal self image, and causes the release of achievement motivation.

Interestingly, the ancient Chinese symbol for stress consists of two pictograms, one over the other. The top one represents "crisis" whilst the bottom one represents "opportunity". The Chinese believe that a situation is just that, a situation, but the way we perceive it turns it either into a crisis or an opportunity.

Those who have goals will discover that there are lots and lots of opportunities out there just waiting to be discovered.

All it takes is to have the goals in the first place, and then they will become aware of the opportunities.

Positive people tend to attract others, and when they are seen as "can-do" people they also attract opportunities to themselves.

Those that preach from the "can't do" gospel however, tend to push people away from them.

There is one other area in which the type of motivation makes a significant impact and that is time management.

Those individuals who benefit through achievement motivation find that they are highly proactive in their approach.

They find themselves able to plan more effectively, and can deal with interruptions and sidetracking extremely well.

Generally they are more assertive overall.

Individuals driven by avoidance motivation however tend to be more re-active, finding their ability to plan quite restricted and that their plans invariably go out of the window on a regular basis.

They are more prone to interruption and being sidetracked than their counterparts, and overall their level of performance is lower.

For all those who set their goals and enjoy the release of achievement motivation, there is one other hugely significant benefit to be obtained.

Because of their approach, they gain access to very powerful areas within their own brains that lie dormant until awakened, and which then go to work on their behalf.

Happy are those who dream
dreams and are prepared to
pay the price to make them
come true.

Leon J Suenes

Chapter 4 - The Power of the Brain.

Neurologists, those very fine specialists who work with the brain, and other researchers, tell us that we humans only use something like 5 – 10% of the brains capacity.

This may be because we only need to use this amount for our purposes, whilst body maintenance uses the rest, or it may be that we have just never learned to put our brains to best use.

Whatever they mean, it is certain that most individuals do not make full use of what is available to them, simply because they do not understand what is available to them and they do not take appropriate action to access it all.

If you have travelled over reasonably long distances by car you will probably be familiar with two travel games, I-Spy and The Yellow Car Game.

In the I-Spy game, one player identifies an item by its first letter, and the rest of the players try to guess it.

Obviously this game works best when played amongst a group of individuals who can spell properly, although it can be very interesting playing it with young children who are just learning to spell and spell phonetically!

The point about this game is about just how many items there are that can be found in the confined space of a car, all beginning with the same letter, and just how many individual items you can recognise that were there already which you were not consciously aware of until the game began.

Perhaps this is better explained through the Yellow Car Game. Statistically there are supposed to be fewer yellow cars on the road than any other colour.

Apparently this is because they have a poorer resale value in view of the colour which makes them unpopular with the masses.

In the yellow car game, players watch for yellow cars and shout "Yellow Car" when they see one.

*The power of imagination
makes us infinite.*

John Muir

The first person to see a yellow car and shout out gets to carry out an "unpleasant" task on fellow players.

This normally involves inflicting pain on the others through a punch or slap, and because of this the rules are quickly changed by responsible adults.

Once the game begins, many yellow cars will be seen, making for a very noisy game.

The big question is where were the yellow cars before the game began? Were there any, or did they "suddenly appear" after the game started?

We will find out the answer to that a little later, but to begin with we need to start a simple exploration of the brain, in order to understand how people use their brains in normal everyday life, and what they are missing out on.

To begin with, imagine that the human brain is like a peeled orange, with 5 segments. The surface is slightly knobbly and there is a covering of thin white fibres all over it.

Each of these segments represents a specific part of the brain, and most people only use 3 of them on a regular basis.

These three are the conscious, pre-conscious and sub-conscious segments. The white fibrous "spiders web" represents the neural network, a series of connections along which energy and thoughts pass.

Conscious Segment

The conscious segment is where we experience things that are going on in other segments or are processed by our senses.

This is the part of our brain that we use to concentrate, experience thinking and structure our language.

It is where we are aware of what is happening.

There is only one true success
in life — to be able to spend
your life in your own way.

Christopher Morley

As you are reading these words, if you are concentrating on them and your mind has not wandered off on a daydream, then you are using your conscious mind.

When you are problem solving or analysing, your awareness of what you are doing is in your conscious segment.

This segment is generally reckoned to be able to deal with only one thing at a time, so that when you are daydreaming and your conscious mind is absorbed in that activity, that is all you can concentrate on.

The conscious segment uses up a lot of energy to process information, and can lead to mental fatigue at the end of a day of hard concentration.

The best way to make use of it is to make sure you concentrate on one thing at a time, as opposed to trying to do too many things at once, which drains mental energy faster as well as creating mental confusion and chaotic thinking.

The Preconscious Segment

This segment appears to be part of our primitive survival mechanism and is an adaptation that enables us to free up our conscious segment by enabling routine, repetitive actions to be dealt with elsewhere.

In so doing, it keeps the conscious mind free and energised for when it might be needed.

The pre-conscious segment can multi-task with known actions, and is reckoned to be able to deal with anything up to 9 different things at any one time.

For example, a car driver who is travelling over a familiar route will tend to drive using their preconscious mind, like being on auto pilot.

They do not have to think about it and can carry on a fluid and fluent conversation with a passenger at the same time.

This segment is sometimes referred to as the "auto-pilot", and that is a very good way to

The only way to find the
limits of the possible is to go
beyond them into the
impossible.

Arthur C Clarke

think of it. It is a way in which we can deal with highly repetitive tasks without having to think about them.

Unfortunately, the downside of this segment is that we can often take habitual action without thinking about it, which can lead to the perpetuation of a situation or situations that we would rather not be in.

It is only later that we realise that we have "done it again!"

The Sub-Conscious Segment

The sub conscious segment is also referred to by some as the unconscious segment.

This is the part of our brain which handles our memory, life support systems and many other things.

However, we are totally unaware of all that goes on in this area because it happens "unconsciously".

There are three main occasions that we are aware of where we tap into our subconscious on a regular basis.

The first of these is when we attempt to recall something from our memory banks.

When we "remember" something we store it away in part of our subconscious mind.

When we need to find it again, a procedure known as recall, our conscious segment sends a trigger into our sub-conscious, asking it to retrieve the piece of stored information.

That piece of information enters our awareness the moment it enters our conscious segment, and we treat it as us having "remembered" it.

In fact what we have done is recalled what we earlier remembered and stored.

The second is when we dream during periods of sleep. Dreams originate deep in the sub-conscious but are experienced in the

conscious mind where they create a reality
for us.

Some analysts believe that dreams emanate
from issues that are stored deep in the
subconscious, perhaps that we are unaware
of, to try and bring them back into our
conscious memories.

Whether that is right or not I do not know,
but the conscious is where we experience
whatever is going on.

The third time we access our sub-conscious
segment is during periods of brainstorming."
This is a technique intended to create a free
flowing out-pouring of ideas and information
in order to plumb the depths of the memory
and get information that the sub-conscious
has linked by some form of connectivity.

What happens when we brainstorm a topic is
that our sub-conscious supplies ideas and
thoughts to our conscious segment based
upon those connections that are made at the
sub-conscious level.

Victory belongs to him most
persevering

Napoleon Bonaparte

This connectivity is not always apparent from the conscious level, but it does exist at much deeper levels, and is the source of a lot of great innovation.

During brainstorming the subconscious scans the memory banks looking for any type of connectivity between stored memories and the topic being brainstormed, regardless of how tenuous, and sends the information to the "surface," where it enters our awareness.

These three segments of the brain are in common use by everyone to a greater or lesser degree every day during normal life.

However, there are two other segments that can and do have a powerful impact on performance and achievement, but to do so they have to be accessed in a particular way.

Otherwise they simply lie dormant and contribute nothing.

The first of these is the creative sub-conscious.

The Creative Sub-Conscious

The segment known as the creative sub-conscious is in reality a subsection of the sub-conscious region of the brain. However it has a particular peculiarity associated with it in that it lies dormant until it is triggered into action.

The creative sub-conscious is a part of the brain that supplies both creative ideas and solutions to enable us to achieve a specific result or solve a particular problem.

It does so by a process of "problem" analysis, followed by a supply of ideas that might fit.

When individuals set meaningful goals for themselves, this area is accessed and works on finding ways to achieve those goals.

Not all the ideas are necessarily ideally suited, but they are ideas that can be worked on.

It is important to realise that this segment quietly works away in the background at its

They can because they
think they can.

Virgil

own speed, and produces its outputs at its own pace.

As an example of how this part of the brain works, if you have ever met someone and been unable to remember their name, only to have their name pop into the conscious segment sometime later, then you have experienced the working of your creative sub-conscious.

Similarly if you have ever put something in a "safe place" and been unable to find it, only to "suddenly remember" some time later where it is, then your creativity has been at work, albeit in a slightly different way.

The creative sub-conscious is only triggered by goal setting, and when you are determined to remember someone's name, that is what you have done – set a goal.

Having a dream or making a wish does not affect it and bring it out of hibernation which

Press on! A better fate awaits you!

Victor Hugo

is why dreams and wishes remain as what they are.

Reticular Activating System

The fifth segment is the reticular activating system or RAS for short.

The RAS is in effect part of our primitive survival mechanism, and its purpose is to prevent our brains being overloaded with irrelevant information, by acting as a filter.

It only allows through information that is important to us and to our survival, whilst at the same time filtering out anything that is not important.

Do you remember the yellow car game I talked about earlier? How many yellow cars did you see before you started playing the game?

The answer is probably none.

They were there however, but until playing the game gave them some sort of importance, your RAS simply filtered them out of your awareness.

It is the same with the I-Spy game. Until you had to try and guess the word, you would be unaware of all the individuals things there were in the interior of the car or seen on the journey.

Interestingly, you would have physically seen them, but they would have been filtered out of your awareness, until you needed to register them in your conscious segment in order to play the game.

There have been many experiments and exercises to demonstrate how we can be disadvantaged by this mechanism, and they show without fail how the RAS filters out information, and prevents us from recognising it until and unless it has some importance attached to it for us.

One way to do this is through goal setting. By goalsetting the RAS can be modified to

Effort only fully releases its reward after a person refuses to quit

Napoleon Hill

allow information to pass through, and by doing that we can then become aware of opportunities that otherwise we just would not have seen.

As a consequence of this, we have more chance of achieving our goal.

As an example, if someone is picking you up from a railway station and they say they will be driving a blue Volvo estate, then you might be surprised at just how many of them you will see in the car park.

Similarly, if you go out and buy one, you will be surprised at just how many there already are on the road.

Ironically, one of the reasons that many individuals fail to pursue their goals is that they cannot see a way to achieve them from the outset, and therefore they do not proceed.

Unfortunately, when the goal is cancelled at inception, the RAS stays closed to ideas and there is no second chance.

The only way to create a channel through the RAS is by setting the goals first in the way already described, and then you will start to "see" opportunities that are already there!

The Whole Brain

Success and achievement are "whole brain" activities, requiring us to utilise all five segments of our brain. We cannot be truly successful with only three segments because we are unable to harness the full power of the brain.

The key to high achievement and all success lies in setting yourself some really challenging goals that will stretch and grow you. Once you do that in the right way, things will begin to happen for you that you never dreamed possible and you can move forward as far as you want to, one step at a time.

There are only two things you cannot predict and they are how successful you can be, and how long it will take.

If you can't imagine the future, you won't create it.

Professor Gary Hamel

The limit to success is often self-imposed, limited by what and how you think.

We were all born to win and then taught to lose, and we can only be as successful as we allow ourselves to be.

As long as we can learn we can continue to develop and the only limiting factors to our growth will be our knowledge and desire.

When it comes to timescales, none of us can control time. What we can do is control activities in order to make best use of time.

In my experience, people who set meaningful and challenging goals invariably achieve them well within the time they themselves have allocated.

This is particularly true for medium and long term goals, rather than short term goals.

Typically, a five year goal will be achieved within 3 or 4, and a ten year goal will be achieved in around 7.

Remember that both of these examples relate to individuals who are determined to achieve their goals, and work at them.

Chapter 5 - Linear Time Management

It does not matter how big your goals are, or how many you set for yourself, because until you make things happen, nothing will happen. That means you have to make time to make things happen, and specifically the right things. That requires you to carry out two very important tasks.

The first of these is to identify what is important to you personally in all aspects of your life, specifically in regard to your future and what you want from it. These things need to be prioritised against everything else.

The second thing is to identify what time you have available to carry out the tasks required to achieve what you have already identified as being important.

Those two things are key to your success, and in themselves define time management, because that is not about what you do, but about how you organise yourself to do what you do.

That is what makes effective time managers effective.

The question is how do you arrive at the point of being well organised in order to make things happen?

There are a number of things you need to do. Firstly, you need to identify all the things that are important to you in all areas of your life.

These would include your personal goals and your business targets as well as family, social and leisure aspects.

The next stage is to make some very basic decisions in terms of how important each area is to you in terms of what it adds to your enjoyment of life.

The reason for this is that if you are a normal, fully functioning person then you probably cannot do everything you might like to.

You therefore have to make some decisions about what you will do, and also what you

One who fears failure limits
his activities. Failure is
only the opportunity to
start again more
intelligently.

Henry Ford

will drop.

There is no point trying to do everything.

As part of this process you need to include not only the short term, but the medium and long term also, because when you come to schedule your activities you need to allocate time to all three time horizons.

All the things that are important to you will require some form of action to either maintain them as they are, or to create them if they are new, like goals for example.

Typically you might find that 65% of your time is going to become occupied with short term oriented activities, around 20% with medium term activities and 15% with long term activities.

The best place to capture all these activites is a to-do list.

Now, some imagine a to-do list to be a sheet of paper on which you write endless lists of things, some of which never get done.

In all honesty if you adopt that approach, you will probably end up creating high levels of personal stress.

A real to-do list is actually a very sophisticated planning tool through which complex tasks, goals and projects are translated into actions.

Remembering that actions are what make things happen, part of the planning process should involve identifying what needs to be done so it can be incorporated into a work or activity schedule.

Most of the individuals that I have met seem to be constantly bombarded with requests for help through the supply of information and for help and assistance.

In the majority of cases, these requests are often outside the area of responsibility of the individuals concerned, and they get caught up because of their inability to say "No".

Part of the reason for this inability is their poor personal organisation and lack of identified priorities. The effective to do list therefore needs to contain the following information:

1. The high level goal or objective – what it is you are trying to achieve.

2. Sub-goals and sub-objectives. Most big goals can be broken down into smaller goals which are often easier to manage, and these sub-levels can be used to identify where time needs to be invested in activity.

3. A priority allocated to each of the actions identified, based upon the importance of the high level goal.

4. A date by which the activity must be completed.

5. The latest time by which the activity can be started and meet its completion deadline

There are several sophisticated diary systems on the market that can be used to manage the type of demands described above.

Alternatively you can use ordinary sheets of A4 paper.

Later on I will describe what I call "3 Sheet Time Management", which is very simple yet very effective.

Once you know what you are trying to manage from your to-do list, you need to think about when you are going to do it.

There are 168 hours in a week, and after deducting time for rest, leisure, travel etc there are around 40 hours remaining.

This is time that is normally allocated to working, and it is during this time that activity should be devoted to the achievement of work goals.

Nothing is easier than being busy – nothing more difficult than being effective

David Clark

Personal goals should be worked on during the hours of leisure, and for this reason it is important to keep the balance right between the two.

However, there is something else that needs to be considered at this point, because it is critical to success.

Most people see time as one-dimensional, and that is through the dimension I call vertical time.

Vertical time is the one we are most familiar with, and it is where we live our lives on a daily basis, and where we experience both living, and the quality of that life.

However, vertical time is an illusion - a man-made device constructed to enable us to be able to work with time in a structured way.

We refer to it as "the present."

There is another, more real, dimension to time, which I call "linear time," and vertical time is simply minute chunks of linear time that have been grouped together in a way that allows us to measure the passage of time in minutes, hours, days, weeks, etc.

We have simply organised these chunks of linear time into larger chunks for our own benefit.

Conveniently for us, these chunks fall into alternate periods of light and darkness as we follow the circadian cycle of day and night and although all this fits together rather well, it actually conspires against us.

Linear time on the other hand is different, very different.

It is raw time or true time, and it breaks all the existing and traditional conventions about time itself.

Traditional conventions assert that we have a past, present and future.

The past is where we have been and lies behind us, the future is where we are going and lies ahead, and the present is where we are now.

But what exactly is the present?

Does it include yesterday, or all of today?

Is tomorrow part of the present or is that part of the future?

The principles of linear time define time completely differently, and in a more accurate and realistic manner.

The best way to think of linear time is as a continuum that stretches far back to a point where time began, wherever that is, and into the future, to infinity.

Our life is spent whilst we journey along the continuum.

The start point of that journey is when we are born, and the end point of the journey is when we die.

What lies between those two points is our life.

We are continuously in motion along the continuum of linear time, rather like the blip on the screen of a heart monitor.

However, there is no present!

As we travel along the continuum, wherever we are on it is a true moment in time which represents the point where the future transforms into the past.

To try and explain how this happens, think of a normal analogue watch with a second hand.

Most of these traditional everyday watches have a second hand that sweeps round the face, pausing every second on a second mark, sixty times a minute.

Although this is on a very small scale, that pause represents the illusion of "the present". Scaled up we can create bigger chunks of the

Our life is what our thoughts make it.

Marcus Aurelias

"present" measured by hours, days and weeks etc.

If on the other hand, you look at a very expensive high-end watch then you come across a different type of movement – one where the second hand sweeps around without pausing, in a very smooth, continuous sweep, and there are no stoppages.

That is what happens with linear time – the transition from the future to the past is smooth, as demonstrated by the expensive second hand.

There is no "present".

So what is the implication for this on the way we manage ourselves and our time?

Simply this - the power to create our own future lies within each and every one of us,

Practitioners of linear time management invest time to reflect on what has gone by, and to learn from it.

Using that learning they are then in a position to make informed decisions and to plan for change if appropriate.

That planning enables them to design and create a different future.

Those who only work in a single dimension with vertical time also design their own future.

However, they invariably do so simply by repeating what they did in the past, because they tend to believe that they are a victim of circumstances without realising that the circumstances are often of their own making.

What makes linear time management so successful can be summed up in the phrase "investing time today to make tomorrow better." Santayana once said "those who ignore history are condemned to repeat it", and that is exactly what happens when individuals are caught up in single dimensional time management.

No bird soars too high if he
soars with his own wings

William Blake

Part of the reason for single dimension time management is that those who experience it are invariably driven by avoidance motivation.

They are so caught up with trying to get through their workload they do not even stop to check whether they should be doing it all or not.

They seem to hold the mistaken belief that someone will come along, hopefully sometime soon, and make everything better for them.

Unfortunately for them, practitioners of single dimensional or vertical time management are unable to break out of the self perpetuating cycle they have created for themselves

Linear time management however enables us to manage our time in a completely different way, and to exercise control over our destinies.

I once came across a definition of insanity which stated the following: "Insanity is the state of mind that exists when you keep on doing the same old things whilst at the same time you keep hoping that something different will happen."

That describes the situation vertical time managers find themselves in every day.

Linear time managers on the other hand see the accomplishment of their goals as the foundation of their personal time management strategies, and the achievement of those goals forms the basis of how they occupy their vertical time.

As part of their strategy, linear time managers do something else that is also very important – they make themselves their top priority. You will need to do the same.

There are a few very good reasons for doing this.

Fatigue makes cowards of us all.

Abraham Lincoln

Firstly, it will enable you to enjoy the proven benefits provided by achievement motivation.

Secondly, you will be able to access those powerful areas that already exist in your brain and use them to your personal advantage.

Thirdly it will give a context to your life into which everything else will fit.

Finally, you will be able to create a prioritisation framework that will enable you to prioritise all your activities in order to ensure that you take care of yourself and your own needs first.

Initially this might sound to be a very selfish approach. However, unfortunately for you, unless and until you do that, you are not taking good care of yourself.

Consequently, if you do not take good care of yourself, then you are not in the best position to deal effectively with, and provide benefit to, others.

The next step in linear time management is to ensure that you allocate some "quality" time to yourself each and every day that you can use for your personal planning.

The best time to do this is towards the end of the day before you switch off for the evening.

This chunk of time is "self management" time, and you should use it to review what has gone before and to reflect on how well you are doing performance wise.

Did you achieve all you set out to? If not, why not?

As part of this you need to look at how closely the actual events of the day compared with what you had planned to achieve.

If the actual events were significantly different to those you had planned you need to find out two things.

The first is why it happened the way it did, and the second is to see if this was a unique occasion due to exceptional circumstances prevailing, or part of a growing trend.

What you find will determine whether you can and should do anything about it.

Then, you plan for the future. This involves looking at the existing workload you already know about, as well as looking to the future to identify things you are going to have to deal with in the short, medium and longer term.

You also need to include actions that you are going to take to prevent a repetition of things you have already identifed as needing to change.

This "management time" is the single most important key to all your future success, because it will enable you to make sure that you are keeping yourself on track and moving in the right direction.

Not only that, but if you should find that you are not going in the right direction, you will

To become what we are
capable of becoming is the
only end in life.

Robert Louis Stevenson

be able to plan what corrective action you need to take and make it happen.

When you see a ship sailing at sea, there is virtually always someone on watch to make sure it is going where it is supposed to be going.

Imagine what might happen if they only popped up every hour or two for a quick glance around to make sure everything was alright.

You wouldn't be comfortable with that idea, particularly if you were a passenger, yet you probably allow it to happen to yourself in your own life on a regular basis.

Worse than that, you may possibly do nothing to change it!

Remember that if you don't know what you want from life, and take steps to achieve it, then you may find yourself not wanting what you do end up with – whatever that may be!

The world is full of opportunities – all sorts
of opportunities, but the reality is you are
probably too busy to look for them. In any
case, until you set your goals, you won't even
see them – because your brain will filter them
out.

If you are reading this book because you
want things to change, then there is only one
way to make it happen.

Practice the management of your linear time.

Make sure you set time aside to think. Use
your thinking time to review the past, and
think about what you have liked, and not
liked.

Do you really want to repeat the past as it
happened? Or are their bits you want to
change? Think about what you really want,
not what you don't want.

Paul J Meyer, one of the great motivational
writers and speakers of the 1970's said in a
speech I listened to "be careful what you
think about, as you will surely get it."

Men do less than they ought,
unless they do all they can.

Thomas Carlyle

Focus your thoughts on what you want to achieve, not on what you want to avoid. That is what is meant by "positive thinking" in its purest form. Design the future you really want, and then use your newfound time and self management skills to create it.

Otherwise you run the risk that you will simply perpetuate the very circumstances that you seek to escape. So how do you set about making this all happen? You plan what you want to do, and then do it. It is that simple.

Firstly you need to begin with your goals, the things you want to achieve.

Secondly, you need to devise your strategies – these relate to how you intend to achieve your goals.

Finally you identify what actions you are going to take in implementing your strategies, and schedule them into your vertical time.

I devised a very simple yet effective way that I call "3 Sheet Time Management".

It involves three sheets of paper that need to be as big as they need to be. You may find A4 paper is big enough, or you might like to use sheets of flip-chart paper.

On the first sheet you will write out all your goals, together with a plan for their achievement. It does not matter at this stage whether the plan is complete in itself or just the initial steps.

The second sheet is your to-do list. Here you will list all the actions you need to take and the activities you will be involved in to achieve, or move towards the achievement, of your goal. Once you have your list prepared you need to prioritise the individual items in the order of their importance, starting with the most important at number 1 and working your way down the list.

The last sheet of paper will be your schedule. On this you will allocate time that you have identified as being available to do the things you have on your to-do list, beginning with

Fools wander but wise men travel.

Confucius

the most important. Obviously you will not be able to do everything at the same time or indeed everything on your list if it is a long one or the actions complex.

However, your prioritisation system will provide you with a sequence of events that you can follow, which will ensure that you are always working on the most important tasks.

Remember, you only have a finite amount of time each day, so you have to be selective about what you choose to do. And don't forget your own management time – the time you will use to reflect, learn and plan.

Unless you manage your time in both dimensions, you run the risk of being driven by avoidance motivation, which means you will end up being driven by events. Once this happens you will find yourself being very reactive, and you run the risk of your own goals and needs taking second place to everything and everyone else.

Be prepared – put yourself first.

Whatever happens to us in
life is a result of the choices
we make, either consciously
or unconsciously

David Clark

Chapter 6 - In Conclusion…………

I started out by asking why some people seemed to achieve so much more than others or to attract more "luck" to themselves. The reason was given as being because they shared a set of common characteristics.

If you remember, they were the following:

- They know what they want

- They are motivated in the appropriate way

- They organise themselves and their time through effective planning to be able to achieve their goals

- They access some very powerful parts of the brain which lie dormant until triggered by goals being set.

You now know what is involved in high levels of personal achievement. You also know what it will take in much more detail than when you set out to read this book.

Hopefully you realise it is available to everyone, including you. It is now down to you to apply it and to make things happen.

Remember however that there will always be challenges and obstacles in the way, and the journey may not be easy – achieving something worthwhile never is.

So, where do you start?

Start by taking time to decide what you want the future, your future, to look like, and set yourself some goals. Make sure that you are clear about what you want, as opposed to what you don't want.

There are two reasons for this.

Firstly because if you follow the steps laid out in this book you will end up with what you create for yourself, and once that happens there is no going back.

Secondly if you don't set out to define what it is that you want, you will have to accept what you get, which you may not want.

The next stage is to make sure that you create time for yourself in order to manage your linear time. This time will be used for review, reflection and planning in order that you can keep moving in whatever direction you want to.

Remember also that time management is not so much about what you do, but about how you organise yourself to do what you do.

When you allocate time to planning you invest in linear time, and when you carry out actions you spend vertical time! They say that the biggest investment you will ever make is in your own property. I think they are wrong.

I believe the biggest investment you will ever make is in time for yourself to plan your own life. You can live anywhere, but you only have one life.

Once you have set your goals and objectives, and allocated time to yourself as part of your

Nothing is easier than being busy – nothing more difficult than being effective.

David Clark

planning, providing you take action then you will see things start to happen.

You will feel more positive about yourself, and feel more confident. You will see more opportunities, and you will begin to "attract luck" to yourself. You will also see yourself begin to move towards the achievement of your goals.

You now have all the information and tools that you need to go out and achieve what you want. All you need now are three sheets of paper and a pen, and you can be underway.

It is your choice that counts.

If you really want to create a different tomorrow, you have to prevent yourself from re-creating today. That means you need to do something different, which will probably feel uncomfortable.

However, your destiny lies in your hands, and whatever decision you make, make sure that what you end up with is what you want.

Life is a journey that we enjoy whilst we are travelling along the continuum of time.

It has many possible destinations, and the life we lead is the consequence of the choices we make along the way.

Everything you do, every single choice you make contributes to where you end up.

You cannot "not" contribute, just as you cannot "not" make a choice.

What you get is what you create for yourself, consciously or unconsciously.

Today is your current destiny – the consequence of all your previous choices. Tomorrow will be also. Except you will be a little further down the linear time continuum.

Time is running out so hurry, and set about creating the future you want.

It's your choice.

Good luck

What the mind can conceive
and believe, it can achieve

Napoleon Hill

NOTES: Now that you have finished reading, make a few key notes here about what you want to achieve with your life. Do it now!

Recommended Reading List.

A selection of books you may care to choose from.

BUSINESS / PERSONAL DEVELOPMENT:

Alpha Plan - David Lewis
Asserting Yourself - Lineham & Egan
Assertiveness At Work - D R Stubbs
Awaken The Giant Within - Tony Robbins
Body Language - Alan Pease
Body Language - Dr Joseph Braysich
Born To Win - James And Jongeward
Changing The Game - Larry Wilson
Effective Performance Appraisals - R B Maddox
Effective Problem Solving - Dave Francis
Effective Teambuilding - John Adair
Effective Time Management - John Adair
Games People Play - Eric Berne
Getting To Yes - Fisher & Ury
Going For It - Victor Kiam
How To Be An Even Better Manager – 1 + 2 - Michael Armstrong

How To Develop Your Personal
Management Skills - June Allan
I Can - Ben Sweetland
I'm O.K. - You're O.K. - Thomas and Amy
Harris
Introducing Neuro-Linguistic Programming-
O'Connor & Seymour
Journey Of Awakening - Ram Dass
Leadership And The One Minute Manager -
Blanchard, Zigami And Zigami
Leadership Skills For Women - Manning
And Haddock
Live Your Dreams - Les Brown
Magic Of Thinking Big - David J. Schwartz
Magic Of Thinking Success -   "   "
Making The Most Of Your Mind - Tony
Buzan
Man's Search For Meaning - Victor Frankl
Management Teams - Why The Succeed Or
Fail - Meredith Belbin
Managing Negotiations - Kennedy, Benson
And McMillan
Maximum Personal Energy - Knutzleman
Mindmapping - Joyce Wycoff
Not Bosses But Leaders - John Adair

One Minute Manager Builds High
Performance Teams - Blanchard And Parisi -
Carew
Positive Workaholism - Dennis Hensley
Psycho - Cybernetics - Maxwell Maltz
Pulling Your Own Strings - W Dyer
Relax: Dealing With Stress - Watts & Cooper
Self Managing Teams - R Hicks And D Bone
Staying Ahead Of Time - Dennis Hensley
Staying O.K. - Amy & Thomas Harris
Stress For Success - Dr Peter Hanson
Success Through A Positive Mental Attitude
- Hill & Stone
Successful Negotiators Handbook - David
Farmer
Super Confidence - Gael Lindenfield
T A Today - Ian Stewart And Vann Joines
Tactics - Edward De Bono
Talk It Out - Daniel Dana
Teamroles At Work - M Belbin
The 10 Day Relaxation Plan - Dr Eric
Trimmer
The Art Of War - Sun Tzu
The Creative Manager - Roger Evans & Peter
Russel
The Hidden Advantage In Selling - Donald J.
Moine & John H. Herd

The Joy Of Stress -   "   "
The One Minute Manager - Blanchard And
Johnson
The One Minute Manager Meets The
Monkey - Blanchard And Lorber
The Psychology Of Interpersonal Behaviour -
Michael Argyle
The Steps To Self Development - Tom Jaap
The Success System That Never Fails - W.
Clement Stone
The Tao Of Leadership - John Heider
The Tao of Coaching – Max Lansberg
Effective Coaching – Marshall J Cook
The Tao Of Management - Bob Messing
The Tao Of Peace - Diane Dreher
Think And Grow Rich - Napoleon Hill
Time Trap - Alec McKenzie
Understanding Organisations - Charles
Handy
Unlimited Power - Anthony Robbins
Use Your Head - Tony Buzan
What Do You Say After You Say Hello? -
Eric Berne
What Do You Say When You Talk To
Yourself - Shad Helmstetter

Printed in the United States
84472LV00002B/22/A

9 781846 858093